LOOKING AT PAINTINGS

Dancers

Isadora Duncan
Antoine Bourdelle, Pen and ink, 1909

LOOKING AT PAINTINGS

Dancers

Peggy Roalf

Series Editor
Jacques Lowe

Designer
Amy Hill

Hyperion Books for Children

A
JACQUES LOWE
VISUAL ARTS PROJECTS
BOOK

Text Copyright © 1992 Jacques Lowe Visual Arts Projects Inc.

Printed in Italy

FIRST EDITION

1   3   5   7   9   10   8   6   4   2

LIBRARY OF CONGRESS CATALOGING-IN-PUBLICATION DATA
Roalf, Peggy
Dancers/Peggy Roalf—1st ed.
p.   cm. — (Looking at Paintings)
"A Jacques Lowe Visual Arts projects book"—T.p. verso
Summary: Presents 2,000 years of art history through a series of
paintings of dancers and the dance.
ISBN 1-56282-089-3 (trade)—ISBN 1-56282-090-7 (lib.bdg.)
1. Dancers in art—Juvenile literature.   2. Dancing in art—
Juvenile literature.   3.Painting—History—Juvenile literature.
[1. Dancers in art. . 2. Dancing in art.   3. Painting—History.
4. Art appreciation.]   I. Title.   II. Series: Roalf, Peggy.
Looking at paintings
ND1460.D34R6   1992
758'.97928—dc20   91-73827
CIP
AC

Contents

Introduction

*L*OOKING AT PAINTINGS is a series of books about understanding what great artists see when they paint. Painters have been attracted to the movement and the excitement of the dance for more than 2,000 years. By looking at many paintings of this one subject, we see how these artists have brought their personal vision of dancers to life, using talent and imagination

Painters are creative explorers. They use their feelings about the world around them to decide what to paint and how to use their materials. Gifted artists can look at something as simple as a playground dance and create a unique painting with light, color, and movement. With their singular power of observation, they can find something unusual in everything they see and often create revolutionary painting techniques to express their point of view.

We will see that Henri Matisse revealed the powerful energy in a circle dance by using bold lines and three brilliant colors, in *The Dance*. Henri de Toulouse-Lautrec watched a graceful figure and captured pure movement with a luminous swirl of color, in *Loie Fuller in the Dance of the Veils at the Folies-Bergères*. Georges Seurat created a new way of painting with thousands of flickering little dots instead of smooth brush strokes, in *The Can-Can*.

Artists transform what they see into magical images that take us on a journey to earlier times and to distant places. You can learn to observe your own world—your family, your cat, your friends who dance—and use your imagination to see like a painter.

MAENAD WITH STAFF AND TAMBOURINE, about 60 B.C.
Unknown Roman Artist, Fresco (Detail)

Rich people lived like kings in ancient Rome. They built beautiful villas with marble halls and swimming pools and gave big parties. For five days every spring, the Romans stopped working to celebrate the festival of Dionysus, the god of wine. They enjoyed the best food and entertainment from all parts of the Roman Empire. To prove they were cultured, not just wealthy, the Romans hired artists to paint pictures from the stories of their gods and goddesses on the walls of their villas. The story of Dionysus and his followers, who were called maenads, was perfect for a house near Pompeii. In A.D. 79, the great volcano of Mt. Vesuvius erupted and buried the city of Pompeii under molten lava. The lava sealed in everything it touched, so many villas and their paintings were saved from the destruction of time.

Maenads were always pictured carrying ivy-topped staffs and tambourines. They worshiped Dionysus with music and wild dancing in the mountain forests. Two thousand years ago, when this mural was created, artists had not yet learned about perspective—how to make the space around their subjects look real—so the maenad figure in this painting seems to float in the air. Even so, the artist used all of his talent to express this vision of beauty. The artist painted with great feeling, using delicate colors and shading to represent the transparency of the dancer's robe floating on the wind as she steps along. The background was painted black so that the maenad would look very bright, as though lit by a spotlight. The Roman painter created this sharp contrast to focus our attention on the dancer's beauty.

Five hundred years before the eruption of Mt. Vesuvius, a Greek artist decorated the back of a mirror with a graceful maenad.

8

9

RECEPTION AT THE COURT OF SHAH TAHMASP,
early 17th century
Unknown Persian Artist, Fresco (Detail)

Shah Tahmasp, a king of Persia, knew how to give a party. He put on a lavish feast when Prince Humayūn of India came to visit, and that scene is pictured in this wall painting. Fresco is an ancient method of painting with pure color directly onto a wet plaster wall. There are no extra liquids holding the colors together; when the paint and plaster dry, they become one material instead of one material on top of another (as in oil on canvas). For this reason, we can look at a fresco from any angle and not be distracted by a shiny surface. And since the picture becomes part of the architecture, artists consider fresco to be the ideal method for wall painting.

The artist who created this fresco put many details into the painting to show great luxury, wealth, and power. Mouth-watering fruits spill out of richly patterned bowls. The shah watches over the festivities from a platform, wearing a turban studded with feathers and precious gems. A jewel-encrusted scimitar symbolizes his authority. Palace guards stand by to protect their king, and graceful dancers entertain.

Shah Tahmasp loved art and hired painters, book designers, and potters to create their best work for his palace. His contributions to the arts were remembered by Shah Abbas, who followed him. When Abbas built the Chihil Sitin for official receptions, he decorated the walls with this mural to honor Tahmasp and to remind visitors of the splendor of his own court.

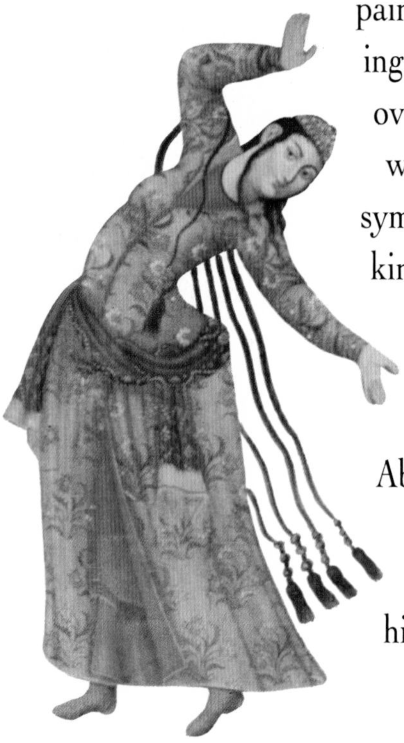

The richly embroidered costumes and intricate hairstyles of this dancer and the one pictured above create a strong focus in the mural.

11

THE WEDDING DANCE, about 1566
Pieter Brueghel the Elder, Flemish (1525/30–1569) Oil on panel, 47" x 62"

More than four hundred years ago, when this picture was painted, farmers toiled from sunup to sundown to eke out a living. At that time political, religious, and civil wars raged in Europe. Worn out by hard labor and the fear of death, the peasants had very few reasons to celebrate. So when there was a wedding, the entire village turned out for a party lasting from dawn until dusk. Pieter Brueghel painted such a festive occasion, with a galloping dance to the music of bagpipes.

There are more than one hundred people in this scene—dancing, drinking, playing tag, and gossiping. Brueghel made all of these activities visible, using color to lead our eyes, little by little, from the bottom of the picture to the top. Patches of red dance from right to left to right and back and the trail of red ends at the top of the picture.

If Brueghel had used *too* much red paint, the activities would have all blended together. So he also used light colors. Brueghel painted blouses and jerkins in golden earth colors. He gave the same pale greenish color of the ground to britches, tunics, and aprons. Brueghel painted these people of the earth with the colors of the earth, using red to guide our eyes through all the events in this big party.

Where is the bride? Find the only woman without a kerchief on her head.

Brueghel painted each dancer's clothing with individual style, as seen in this detail.

12

PEASANTS' DANCE, 1636/40
Peter Paul Rubens, Flemish (1577–1640) Oil on panel, 28 1/4" x 41 3/4"

*P*eter Paul Rubens is known as "the Prince of Painters" because he painted the energy of life into his work. He created majestic portraits of princes and bankers, huge pictures of historical events, and religious scenes for cathedrals. The archduke and archduchess who ruled the Low Countries noticed his great talent, and they hired him to be their official painter.

After thirty years of creating large-scale works for important people, Rubens felt he deserved some time to paint for his own enjoyment. He moved to a country house and spent time outdoors, sketching the natural world and the local farmers.

Inspired by the vision of his countryman Pieter Brueghel (p. 12), Rubens painted his own view of a peasant dance. He captured the farmers' strength and their spirit of fun after a day of hard work. In swirling skirts and glimmering fur jerkins, the peasants dance in a zigzag line that intensifies the feeling of movement in the picture. Each face is an individual portrait, which was Rubens's way of showing his great respect for the peasants' way of life. He painted the dancers' skin using a transparent glaze on top of opaque paint. Rubens's painting technique allowed the colors underneath to shine through, and the peasants' skin glows with a light that seems to shine from within.

In this detail, Rubens shows us that hands can be as expressive as faces.

CARNIVAL SCENE, about 1756
Giovanni Domenico Tiepolo, Italian (1727–1804)
Oil on canvas, 29 3/4" x 47 1/4"

If somebody said to us, "Tell me the difference between *looking* at something and *seeing* something," we might say, "There's no difference." And we would be absolutely wrong.

Giovanni Domenico Tiepolo grew up learning to observe every detail of his surroundings from his father, who was a famous painter named Giovanni Battista Tiepolo. Domenico's eyes were like zoom lenses—he could view what was in front of him as one big picture or zero in on small parts of a scene to notice the difference between the dress of an actress and the dress of a princess.

Domenico's ability to sharply observe the world around him, and then paint a vivid picture of it, made him a popular artist.

Domenico brought an afternoon party in the country to life with action and detail. Events like this one were often held at his family's villa near Venice, and he saw them firsthand. Two professional dancers perform in the foreground while actors in masks and tall hats await their turn. Domenico painted the man's red costume and feathered hat so exactly right that we know the dancer is dressed as a character called Mezzetino. We can easily tell who the guests are because their clothes are plainer than those of the dancers and actors.

Domenico made his painting of the fancy party, lively dance, and silky costumes so lifelike that we can really tell what it was like to be a wealthy Venetian in the 1750s.

Another Italian artist, Pinelli, shows the costumes worn by dancers one hundred years later.

BUGAKU DANCE, about 1720
Hanabusa Itchō, Japanese (1652–1724)
Ink and watercolor on gold leaf, 72 1/8" x 177 5/8"

The painter of this screen was inspired by the Japanese art of fabric design.

Hanabusa Itchō lived in a time of peace and prosperity, when wealthy merchants and military rulers in Japan spent great sums to decorate their mansions and castles. These buildings had enormous rooms that were dark and drafty. Instead of walls to make separate spaces, large movable screens covered with paintings were used to divide the rooms and protect the dwellers from drafts.

These winged figures are on a fifteen-foot-wide screen that illustrates an ancient dance called Bugaku; they prowl, pounce, and stamp their feet to the music on wooden flutes and drums. Itchō used brilliantly colored inks and watercolors for the figures. Because he created the painting as a decoration for a very wealthy person, he first put a film of real gold all over the background. And he knew that light bouncing off the shiny surface would brighten up the room.

Like other great Japanese artists, Itchō found beauty in the spaces between figures. He shaped the golden areas around the dancers and made them just as interesting as the costumes.

Itchō modeled his design on a similar screen painted forty-five years earlier by his teacher, Kano Yasunobu. And Yasunobu got *his* idea by looking at a painting of Bugaku created one hundred years before. Each painter used the work of another artist as a starting point, then made his own original version of the classic dance.

OBERON, TITANIA AND PUCK WITH FAIRIES, DANCING, 1785
William Blake, English (1757–1827) Watercolor on paper, 18 3/4" x 26 1/2"

Illiam Blake was a great poet as well as a painter. He created this watercolor to illustrate a play called *A Midsummer Night's Dream*, which was written by another great English poet, William Shakespeare.

According to legend, on June 21st—the longest day of the year—people do strange and silly things. The play tells the story of two pairs of lovers tricked into falling in love with the wrong partners. Oberon, king of the fairies, ordered his chief sprite, the mischievous Puck, to sprinkle nectar from an enchanted flower into the men's eyes while they slept. On awakening, each falls in love with the first person he sees. After several merry mix-ups are straightened out, Oberon, Queen Titania, and their magical followers celebrate the lovers' weddings—to the right partners. As the play ends, the fairies dance and sing this song before disappearing into their invisible kingdom:

The energetic movements of a circle dance fascinated Nicholas Poussin, who lived two hundred years before Blake.

"Trip away; make no stay:
meet me all by break of day."

William Blake painted the last scene of the play with watercolors. He created velvety deep tones for the mysterious nighttime forest by painting on many layers of color, letting each layer dry in between. Because watercolor paint is transparent, the colors underneath shine through and sparkle like jewels. For the figures, Blake used only a few layers of pale, luminous color, then applied some darker touches of paint for the shadows. He used the magical qualities of watercolor to express the enchantment of midsummer night.

BULL DANCE, MANDAN O-KEE-PA CEREMONY, 1832
George Catlin, American (1796–1872) Oil on canvas, 24 ¼" x 28"

George Catlin had a personal mission. He visited the Great Plains Indians before photography was in common use and painted pictures of their customs to create a unique record. He believed that their native way of life would be destroyed by the white explorers and fur traders who brought a different culture to the tribes.

Catlin often traveled alone through the wild and dangerous western states, carrying his painting supplies on his back. He made friends with the great chiefs, who invited him to live in their villages.

The Bull Dance was part of the most important Mandan tribal ceremony. Eight braves wearing buffalo skins, with willow branches tied onto their backs, and four more with painted bodies and towering headdresses, perform the dance. They ask their god, the Great Spirit, to bring the tribe success in hunting. Catlin painted this scene from atop one of the buffalo-hide lodges to give us a bird's-eye view of the ceremony.

Catlin was a realistic painter who could make a portrait look exactly like its subject. But he painted in a very different way when he portrayed Native Americans. He wanted to make the Indians' unspoiled nature visible, so he used what is known as a "primitive" style of painting. Catlin made the shapes of things simpler than they really were, using bold, almost childlike patches of color. By doing this, he gives us a truthful picture of Native American life that we can understand at a glance.

The Plains Indians believed that magical powers enabled George Catlin to paint a likeness of their chief.

A SUMMER NIGHT, 1890

Winslow Homer, American (1836–1910) Oil on canvas, 29 ½" x 39 ¾"

*I*magine the most glorious night of summer. The full moon rises so high we have to crane our necks to see it. Everybody goes out to watch the brilliant moonlight casting shadows of clouds onto the rolling surf. The boys crowd onto the rocks and sing, "Buffalo gals, won't you come out tonight...and dance by the light of the moon?" as two girls whirl about on the porch. Summer evenings like this were common at Winslow Homer's residence in Maine, and he captured the radiant light in *A Summer Night*.

If we look closely, we can see that Homer put more than one kind of light into this picture. The moonlight behind the people on the rocks makes them look like silhouettes. The bright lamps from the house (which are really in front of the painting) cast long shadows of the dancers onto the porch; in the distance, a red lighthouse beam glimmers on the horizon. Homer used the contrast of warm, bright light and deep, cool shadows to re-create the mood of the most perfect summer night by the sea.

Winslow Homer's studio sat on a cliff above the fierce Atlantic Ocean. He made a charcoal drawing of this night scene on the spot to catch the effect of the different kinds of light. Later, in his small studio on the beach, he had two neighbors pose for the dance. Back in his main studio, he studied his drawings and combined all of his ideas to create this large painting that he had originally called *Buffalo Gals*.

THE DANCE CLASS, 1876
Edgar Degas, French (1834–1917) Oil on canvas, 33 ½" x 29 ½"

The lesson seems endless. And the teacher demands one more try from the ballerina in the middle. The girl with the green bow impatiently flutters her fan, the one next to her yawns and scratches. Even the little dog under the piano looks bored.

Edgar Degas painted with affection an ordinary moment in these dancers' lives. He admired the repeated efforts they made to perfect their movements. And the careful repetition of the dance lessons gave him the opportunity to capture their motion in his drawings.

Degas practiced drawing so much that he developed a photographic memory. He could look at one of his sketches (below) and see in his mind what the dancer would look like turned in any direction. With a very confident hand, he painted the same figure he had sketched, but looking to the right and holding a fan.

In his studio, Degas created this large picture using his memory and sketches to re-create a classroom scene. The steady gaze of the dance master, the great mirror in the center, and the red ribbons and fan of the first dancer focus our attention on the ballerina in the middle. The high ceiling of the classroom makes us realize the importance of this moment. Degas painted a liquid light that bathes the figures in even tones, but he added shadows on the dancers in front to lead our eyes into the action of the painting. By simplifying the details of the dancers' faces and costumes, he helps us feel the nervous energy of the entire group.

Degas used ink and gouache to create this study for the painting opposite.

26

TWO DANCERS ON THE STAGE, 1874
Edgar Degas, French (1834–1917) Oil on canvas, 24 1/4" x 18 1/8"

We are late for the theater! The curtain has gone up! As we scurry in the dark to our seats, wondering what we've missed, we glimpse two dancers on the stage.

This painting looks as though it was quickly dashed off to preserve a memory—like a snapshot. The dancer on the right is "interrupted" by one edge of the painting; on the left, the tutu of a third ballerina pokes into the scene.

Edgar Degas was fascinated by photography. He especially liked the way news photos stop motion and freeze it forever in time. Such pictures were taken in a hurry, and the figures were often cut off at the edges. Degas sensed that things were happening beyond the margins, which make the photos seem real. He used the same approach in this painting.

Degas gave us a bird's-eye view of the stage from high up in the theater. He shortened, or telescoped, the distance between his seat and the performance, putting us right into the action.

The floor is important to a ballerina: she springs into flight from the floor and, there, she gracefully lands. Degas made the floor a large part of this picture, with diagonal stage markings leading straight to the figures. Their costumes gleam and flutter under the bright lights, and the muted tones in the background make the ballerinas stand out even more.

With a few charcoal lines, Degas captured a young dancer's stance.

28

DANCING AT THE MOULIN DE LA GALETTE, 1876
Pierre-Auguste Renoir, French (1841–1919) Oil on canvas, 51 ½" x 68 ⅞"

When Renoir was an art student, he said to his teacher, "I only want to paint the things that I really enjoy." He meant what he said, so his paintings invite us to enter his personal world, where beauty and pleasure are the most important things.

The Moulin de la Galette was a café with a backyard garden where people met for Sunday afternoon dances. In this painting, Renoir included his artist friends and the young women who worked nearby as florists and dressmakers. These were people Renoir knew well, and he made them look carefree and relaxed. The friends posed in Renoir's backyard, which had the same kind of dappled light as the café garden.

Renoir painted colorful glazes over dark areas to create the sparkling effect of sunlight.

Renoir bathed the scene with sunlight sparkling gaily through the trees; the areas of light are filled with color, creating a sense of gaiety. He painted details in the foreground figures to separate them from the background—charming dresses with lace and velvet ribbons, lovely hats and hairstyles, and the men's starched collars. But he painted these details using films of color over color, not with outlines and shading. With quick dashes of paint, Renoir suggests a great crowd in the background, completing the festive scene. After we have studied the painting for a while, we feel that we have become one of Renoir's friends and have joined the party.

LOIE FULLER IN THE DANCE OF THE VEILS AT THE FOLIES-BERGÈRES, 1898
Henri de Toulouse-Lautrec, French (1864–1901) Oil on cardboard

Henri de Toulouse-Lautrec had a passion for sketching. When he was a child, he drew everywhere—in his school notebooks and even in the margins of his dictionary. He was especially good at drawing fast-moving figures.

When he became an artist, Henri went to the theater almost every evening and sketched the dancers and actors. He created theatrical posters and illustrations for magazines, as well as paintings to hang on the wall.

Toulouse-Lautrec was enchanted by Loie Fuller, an American entertainer who created the illusion of dance by standing nearly still under the brilliant stage lights and shifting her long veils of silky material with sticks. She produced a moving cloud of color, and caused a public sensation. With just a few fluid strokes of paint, Toulouse-Lautrec captured the unusual effect of this startling performance.

Toulouse-Lautrec used a special trick to make this oil paint look like pastel painting. He put the paint on blotting paper to soak out most of the oil, then thinned it with turpentine. Because he had removed so much of the oil, the paint dried quickly and the colors had great intensity. The brown cardboard on which he often painted absorbed the colors, adding to the chalklike quality that became Toulouse-Lautrec's "signature."

In a quick sketchbook drawing, Toulouse-Lautrec captured the great strength of a dancer's legs.

33

THE CAN-CAN, 1889–90
Georges Seurat, French (1859–1891) Oil on canvas, 66 ¹/₂" x 54 ¹/₄"

In France, the last decade of the nineteenth century was filled with laughter and cheer to celebrate a period of prosperity after a war that had nearly ruined the country. There was a feeling of optimism about the twentieth century: the Industrial Revolution allowed an easier life for most people, and they had more time for leisure activities. This decade was called La Belle Epoque, which means the beautiful era.

Georges Seurat was inspired by progress and technology, and he developed a "scientific approach" for expressing feelings with colors: red, yellow, and orange meant happiness; brown and gray were for sadness; lavender and blue were for peace.

Seurat loved Parisian nightlife, and he painted a dazzling performance of the can-can using dots of color and simple shapes to express the feeling of fun. Everything about the way he painted this high-kicking dance creates motion—the amused expressions of the performers, the steep angle of the bass violin and the dancers' legs, and the upward glance and raised arm of the conductor. Seurat used the lid of a cigar box for this small oil sketch for a large painting of the same title. He brushed on the colors in soft little blobs that flutter with gaiety, and he put orange dots over all of the bright areas to create a shimmering, happy glow of light.

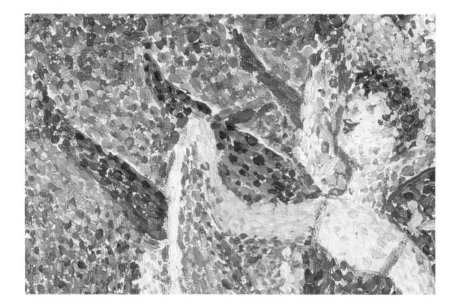

In this detail, we can see how Seurat painted gay orange dots everywhere, even in the shadows.

THE DANCE, 1909
Henri Matisse, French (1869–1954) Oil on canvas, 108" x 144"

"An avalanche of color has no force," said Henri Matisse. So he used only three dominant colors to show the joy of dancing. He used a bright blue for the sky, the greenest of greens for the grass, and a glowing pink for the figures. We feel the energy of the dancers in the bold shapes, rhythmic lines, and brilliant colors. Matisse believed that to show the true spirit of a happening, you had to throw away every mental picture you had of the subject. And this is what he did by using just a few colors and almost no detail.

The dancers whirl in a ring, and the girl in the front has lost her balance. Matisse interrupted the circle of arms and created two different rhythms—the figures on the left are graceful and soaring, the ones on the right are angular and awkward. He drew the dancers with boldly brushed-on lines and let the edges of the painting cut into the scene. Because he appreciated Japanese painting, he used the idea of making the spaces between the figures important, like Itchō had done with the Bugaku dancers on page 19.

Matisse made this painting as a full-size sketch for a picture requested by a Russian art collector. We know from Matisse's letters and diaries that he created it in two days, to instantly capture, with color and design, his feelings about the spirit of the dance.

Matisse also made a charcoal study for The Dance *but changed the form and placement of the figures as he drew.*

CITY ACTIVITIES WITH DANCE HALL, 1930
Thomas Hart Benton, American (1889–1975) Tempera on wood, 92" x 134 ½"

Thomas Hart Benton moved from Indiana to New York City when he decided to be an artist. He wanted to show how ordinary people shaped great events, so he painted murals for city buildings—enormous paintings that would be seen by many people going to work.

For this mural, which depicts a period of industrial growth in America, he traveled through the United States making hundreds of sketches of people in everyday situations: making steel, harvesting wheat, having fun. He pinned the drawings up on the wall of his studio and used his memory and imagination to create a 96-foot-long painting called *America Today*.

Benton separated the scenes in this mural by using contrasting colors and silvery frames.

In this section, four couples dance to jazz music; their motion symbolizes the frantic fun-loving style of the Roaring Twenties, an era that ended with the stock market crash of 1929. Above them, a worried Wall Street broker receives some bad news on his ticker tape.

Benton really knew how to weave stories together with paint. He separated the many different events from each other by using colors that contrast: red and brown next to green and lavender. And he added streamlined silvery frames to lead our eyes from one story to another across the length of the painting. His great talent was met by an unusual opportunity: the federal government hired Benton to paint murals for public buildings through the Work Projects Administration (WPA); this program combined painting with public architecture.

38

DANCING IN COLOMBIA, 1980
Fernando Botero, Colombian (born 1932) Oil on canvas, 74" x 91"

Fernando Botero was born in Colombia, South America, where the enormous Andes Mountains tower over villages and make the houses seem smaller than they really are. Maybe that is why Botero exaggerates the shapes and sizes of the people he paints.

The first thing we notice in this painting is the contrast, or the great difference between things: the towering size of the jazz players and the tiny dancers, the still pose and blank expression of the musicians, and the energy of the couple. The dull colors of the men's clothing makes the red in the neckties and women's clothing seem brighter than it actually is. The band is playing, but the stringed instruments have no strings and the woodwinds no keys!

Botero painted the colors smoothly onto the canvas, leaving no brush marks on its surface. He used many small details to create a "frame" around the painting: bare light bulbs above, cigarette butts and oranges on the floor, and a red curtain. This frame squeezes the figures into the already crowded room and lets us really feel the atmosphere of a hot, smoky party.

In this detail, the missing strings on the guitar and the facial expression of the musicians are clues to Botero's sense of humor.

OPEN-AIR DANCING IN FLORIDA — 1925 (1985)
Oscar de Mejo, American (born in Italy, 1911) Acrylic on canvas, 28" x 34"

Sometimes we have a dream so wonderful that we believe it is real. We struggle to stay asleep and try to reenter the dream. The man who painted this scene gives us a dream from his own childhood.

When he lived with his family in Italy, Oscar de Mejo saw a photograph of a party in Florida, and it stuck in his mind. The photo reminded him of American jazz, his favorite music. De Mejo was a pianist and composer before he became a full-time artist, and he painted this fantasy of an afternoon dance to show what he imagined (when he was a child) American life to be.

De Mejo did something special to make this painting look dreamlike. He repeated many things to make patterns or designs: notice the pattern made by the teapots, cups, and glasses on the tables. The shadows of the people and the palm trees make another pattern on the ground. Most of the people sitting down are doing exactly the same thing—crossing their legs. The children look like small copies of the adults. And the dance itself is a pattern made up of steps that are repeated many times. The little boy at the back of the patio is a self-portrait of the artist as a child, looking at the scene that would stay in his mind forever.

De Mejo exaggerated the differences in the height of the children and the adults.

DANCE OF LOVE, 1987
Grimanesa Amoros, Peruvian (born 1962) Acrylic on canvas, 56" x 46"

Grimanesa Amoros grew up in Peru, where she often saw the Inti Festival at Machu Picchu. Wearing large masks and brilliantly colored costumes decorated with gold, the Quechua peoples celebrated the life-giving power of the sun god. The Indians' contact with the spirit world made a strong impression on Amoros, and colorful images of their pageantry and ritual became a part of her world.

When she went to art school, Amoros was asked to draw human figures and, like the rest of the class, to make them look real—eyes and noses exactly where they belonged, arms and legs that looked just like the models'. Instead, the pictures in her mind flew into her hands, and out came huge, magical people that took over the pages of her drawing pad. Amoros's teacher often scolded her for not following instructions, but, knowing that she *could* make realistic drawings, he was not too harsh.

Amoros uses acrylic paints and large brushes to build up thick layers of clean, quick-drying colors. She always has a vision when she begins, and she paints rapidly, before the spell is broken. In *Dance of Love*, Amoros represented her feelings about life and love. With pale, airy colors and bold, powerful shapes, she painted a boy and girl gliding across the terrace of an enchanted garden, and she stroked on big patches of red from her memories of Machu Picchu.

This drawing was made by Michelle Wild, a young artist who often sketches the dancers whom she sees on the streets of New York City.

Glossary and Index

Abbas, Shah, 10
America Today, 38
Amoros, Grimanesa, 44
ARCHITECTURE, 10, 38: (1) A building that has been carefully
designed and constructed. (2) The art of designing buildings.

BACKGROUND, 8, 18, 28, 30: The part of a painting behind
the subject; the distant area. (See FOREGROUND.)
Benton, Thomas Hart, 38
Blake, William, 20
Botero, Fernando, 40
Brueghel, Pieter, the Elder, 12, 14 (Pronounced Peter Broy-gull):
Brueghel's name is sometimes spelled "Bruegel," to distinguish this
artist from his son, Pieter Brueghel the Younger, who was also a
painter.
Buffalo Gals, 24
Bugaku Dance, 18, 36
Bull Dance, Mandan O-Kee-Pa Ceremony, 22

Can-Can, The, 34
CANVAS, 10, 16, 22, 24, 26, 28, 30, 34, 36, 40, 42, 44: A woven
fabric (often linen or cotton) used as a painting surface. It is usually
stretched tight and stapled onto a wooden frame in order to
produce a flat, unwrinkled surface.
Carnival Scene, 16
Catlin, George, 22
CHARCOAL, 24, 28, 36: A soft, black stick of burned wood, used to
make drawings. Painters use charcoal because it can be blended
and smudged, producing lines and tones of gray, as in a painting,
but in black and white.
CHIHIL SITIN, 10 (Pronounced Chih-hill Sih-tin): In the Farsi
language, it means "The Hall of Forty Columns." A pavilion built
by Shah Abbas in 1660 next to his palace in Isfahan, Iran (then
called Persia); it was used for official dinners and receptions.
City Activities with Dance Hall, 38
CONTRAST, 8, 24, 38, 40: Big differences in light and dark, shapes
and colors.

Dance, The, 36
Dance Class, The, 26
Dance of Love, 44
Dancing at the Moulin de la Galette, 30
Dancing in Colombia, 40
De Mejo, Oscar, 42 (Pronounced Duh May-o)
Degas, Edgar, 26, 28 (Pronounced Deh-gah)
DESIGN, 10, 18, 36, 42: (1) The arrangement of objects and figures in
a painting through the combination of colors and shapes. This is
also called composition. (2) A pattern of shapes on a surface.
DETAIL, 8, 10, 12, 14, 16, 26, 30, 34, 36, 40: (1) Small parts of a
painting, such as objects on a table or decorations on a dress. (2)
When used in a book: a section of a painting enlarged to provide a
close-up view of textures and colors.
DRAWING, 24, 26, 28, 32, 36, 44: The art of creating an image by
making marks on paper. Drawings can be made using dry
materials such as pencil, charcoal, and crayon or wet materials such
as ink and paint. Drawings may consist of lines, tones, shading, and
dots. Twentieth-century artists began to create drawings that are
difficult to distinguish from paintings. An important difference is
that drawings are usually on paper rather than canvas, wood, or
metal. Drawings produced with more than one kind of material are
known as "mixed media" drawings.

FOREGROUND, 16, 30: The area in a painting closest to the viewer.
(See BACKGROUND.)
FRESCO, 8, 10: A method of painting onto wet plaster, usually with
watercolor, to create a picture in which the paint is absorbed into
the wall instead of remaining on the surface.

GLAZE, 14: A transparent, or almost transparent, thinned-down layer
of paint applied over dry paint, allowing the colors underneath to
show through.
GOLD LEAF, 18: Squares of real gold, pounded thinner than paper.
Gold leaf is placed onto a surface coated with tacky adhesive and
carefully pressed into position with soft cotton.

Homer, Winslow, 24

ILLUSTRATION, 32: A drawing or painting created to enhance the
meaning of a text. Illustrations are found in books, magazines,
posters, and newspapers.
INK, 18: Usually, a jet-black fluid made of powdered carbon mixed
with a water-soluble liquid. Ink drawings can be made with dark
lines and diluted tones of gray. Inks are also made in colors and
used in paintings.
Itchō, Hanabusa, 18, 36 (Pronounced Han-a-boos-a Eech-o)

Loie Fuller in the Dance of the Veils at the Folies-Bergères, 32

Maenad with Staff and Tambourine, 8 (Pronounced mee-nad)
Matisse, Henri, 36
Midsummer Night's Dream, A, 20
MURAL, 8, 10, 38: A very large painting that decorates a wall or is
created as part of a wall.

Oberon, Titania and Puck with Fairies, Dancing, 20
OPAQUE, 14: Not letting light pass through. Opaque paints conceal
what is under them. (The opposite of transparent.)
Open-Air Dancing in Florida, 1925, 42

PAINT: Artists have used different kinds of paint, depending on the
materials that were available to them and the effects they wished to
produce in their work.
Different kinds of paint are similar in the way they are made.
1. Paint is made by combining finely powdered pigment with a
vehicle. A vehicle is a substance that evenly disperses the color and
produces a consistency that can be like mayonnaise and sometimes
as thick as peanut butter. The kind of vehicle used sometimes gives
the paint its name. Pigment is the raw material that gives paint its
color. Pigments are made from natural minerals and from man-
made chemical compounds.
2. Paint is made thinner or thicker with a substance called a medium.
Different paints require the use of mediums appropriate to their
composition.

3. A solvent must be used by the painter to clean the paint from brushes, tools, and the hands. The solvent must be appropriate for the composition of the paint.

ACRYLIC PAINT, 42, 44: Pigment is combined with an acrylic polymer vehicle that is created in a laboratory. By itself, acrylic paint dries rapidly. Several different mediums can be used with acrylic paint: Retarders slow the drying process, flow extenders thin the paint, an impasto medium thickens the paint, a gloss medium makes it shiny, a matte medium makes it dull.

Acrylic paint has been popular since the 1960s. Many artists like its versatility and the wide range of colors that are made. Acrylic paint is also appreciated because its solvent is water, which is nonhazardous.

OIL PAINT, 10, 12, 14, 16, 22, 24, 26, 28, 32, 34, 36, 40: Pigment is combined with an oil vehicle (usually linseed or poppy oil). The medium chosen by most artists is linseed oil. The solvent is turpentine. Oil paint dries slowly, which enables the artist to work on a painting for a long time. Some painters mix other materials, such as pumice or marble dust, into oil paint to produce thick layers of color. Oil paint is never mixed with water. Oil paint has been used since the fifteenth century. Until the early nineteenth century, artists or their assistants ground the pigment and combined the ingredients of paint in their studios. When the flexible tin tube (like a toothpaste tube) was invented in 1840, paint made by art suppliers became available.

TEMPERA, 38: Pigment is combined with a water-based vehicle. The paint is combined with raw egg yolk to "temper" it into a mayonnaiselike consistency usable with a brush. The solvent for tempera is water. Tempera was used by the ancient Greeks and was the favorite method of painters during the medieval period in Europe. It is now available in tubes, ready to use. The painter supplies the egg yolk.

WATERCOLOR, 18, 20, 26: Pigment is combined with gum arabic, a water-based vehicle. Water is both the medium and the solvent. Watercolor paint now comes ready to use in tubes (moist) or in cakes (dry). With transparent watercolor, unlike other painting techniques, white paint is not used to lighten the colors. Watercolor paint is thinned with water, and areas of paper are often left uncovered to produce highlights.

Gouache is an opaque form of watercolor, which is also called tempera.

Watercolor paint was first used 37,000 years ago by cave dwellers who created the first wall paintings.

PASTEL, 32: (1) A soft crayon made of powdered pigment, chalk, water, and mixed with a small amount of gum. (2) A painting or sketch made with this type of crayon.

Peasants' Dance, 14

PERSPECTIVE, 8: Perspective is a method of representing people, places, and things in a painting or drawing to make them appear solid or three-dimensional, rather than flat. Turn to page 26, and look at *The Dance Class*, by Edgar Degas, as you read six basic rules of perspective that are used in Western art.

1. People in this painting appear larger when near and gradually become smaller as they get farther away.
2. People in the foreground overlap the activity behind them.
3. People become closer together as they get farther away.
4. People in the distance appear higher up in the picture than those in the foreground.
5. Colors are brighter and shadows are stronger in the foreground. Colors and shadows are paler and softer in the background.

6. Lines that, in real life, are parallel (such as the line of a ceiling and the line of a floor) are drawn at an angle, and the lines meet at the "horizon" line, which represents the eye level of the artist and the viewer. Place a ruler along the line of the ceiling, and another ruler along the line of the floor, and see how Degas used perspective in *The Dance Class*.

Painters have used these methods to represent objects in space since the fifteenth century. But many twentieth-century artists have decided not to use perspective. For example, Henri Matisse expressed his feelings about dancing by using color, lines, and shapes instead of perspective (see page 36).

PHOTOGRAPHY, 22, 28: The art of creating images by exposing light-sensitive film in a camera and creating a print called a photograph through the use of light-sensitive paper and chemicals. In black-and-white work, the result is a negative, in which dark tones appear light and light tones, dark. In the printing stage, the negative is reversed, resulting in a positive image, which is the way the image originally looked. Paper is commonly used in printing, but many other materials, such as steel or canvas, may be made light-sensitive and serve the same purpose as photographic print paper. In color photography, negative-to-positive prints can be made, as well as slides and transparencies, which are positive images produced with what is known as color reversal film.

Painters have made use of camera pictures since the fifteenth century. But it was not until the nineteenth century that the forerunner of the modern camera and a way to prevent photographic prints from fading were perfected by two French inventors, J. Nicephore Niepce and L. J. M. Daguerre.

The modern box camera was introduced by Eastman Kodak in 1888. Kodak's easy-to-use negative paper and readily available processing and printing put photography into general use.

Credits

48